REAL

The Superhero In You™

Sophia Day®

Written by Kayla Pearson   Illustrated by Timothy Zowada

May your childhood be filled with adventure, your days with hope, and your learnings with wisdom, and may you continuously grow as an MVP Kid, preparing to lead a responsible, meaningful life.

-SOPHIA DAY

The Sophia Day® Creative Team-
Kayla Pearson, Timothy Zowada, Stephanie Strouse,
Megan Johnson, Celestte Dills, Patty Lopez Gregersen, Mel Sauder

A **special thank you** to our team of reviewers who graciously give us feedback, edits, and help ensure that our products remain accurate, applicable, and genuinely diverse.

Text and pictures copyrighted ©2021 by MVP Kids Media, LLC

All rights reserved. No part of this publication may be reproduced in whole or in part by any mechanical, photographic, or electronic process, or in the form of any audio or video recording nor may it be stored in a retrieval system or transmitted in any form or by any means now known or hereafter invented or otherwise copied for public or private use without the written permission of MVP Kids Media, LLC.

Published and Distributed by MVP Kids Media, LLC - Mesa, Arizona, USA
Printed in China
Designed by Stephanie Strouse

ISBN 978-1-64786-313-5
DOM Jan 2021, Job #14-004-01

Learning to read
with *The Superhero In You*

Learning how to read is a big, exciting step for children. This book is designed for you to help a child build reading skills. As you read, don't forget to look at the illustrations and discuss what is happening on each page to help increase analyzing skills and comprehension.

You're talented and **capable** of great things. Let your inner superhero fuel your dreams.

The more experienced reader reads the page on the **LEFT SIDE**.

Most importantly, enjoy your time with this book! Children who love to read will find themselves on a path to success. As you read our Mighty Tokens™ series, you are investing in your child's future. Use this book to deposit tokens of affirmation into your children's character, helping them to someday become mighty adults.

The new reader reads the page on the **RIGHT SIDE**.

Learning about **motivation** using **superheroes**

Before you jump into the story, have the more experienced reader read these two pages, and discuss them together.

What is a superhero?

A superhero is someone who helps people and makes the world a better place. You don't need special powers to be a superhero—all you need is the right motivation!

Head for problem-solving.

Ears to listen.

Mouth for kind words.

Hands that help.

Heart ready to serve.

Feet equipped for action.

Watch out for the villains who will try to steal your motivation away!

Professor Failure

El Meaningless Rewardo

Dr. Lazy Stryker

What is motivation?

Motivation is what makes you want to do something. There are two types of motivation.

Outside Motivation vs. Inside Motivation

PRIZES

FAME

DESIRE TO HELP OTHERS

DREAMS

INTERESTS

When making the world a better place is what **YOU WANT** to do, inside motivation is what will make it possible.

Now let's begin the story.

 Tonight is the night of the big celebration. Are you ready to get started?

Yes I am. Look at this!

Do you like it?

 I do like it. It reminds me a lot of you. But what really matters is how you feel about your work. Are you **happy** with it?

I am **happy** with it! It makes me want to do good things.

Then wake up the **superhero** in you, and let it motivate you to always do your best.

I want to be a **superhero**.

I will do my best!

You're talented and **capable** of great things. Let your inner superhero fuel your dreams.

I feel able to do great things.

I am **capable**.

 When you build your skills and learn success, you will feel the satisfaction from your **work**.

I will **work** until the job is really done.

 Watch out for things that try to defeat your inner hero.

Stay away!

I will not let you stop me!

 Professor Failure will try to scare you from trying new **things**, but you don't need to be afraid.

Not today! I am not afraid to try new **things**!

Dr. Lazy Stryker will try to slow you down and make you miss out on **great** things.

Not today! There are too many **great** things for me to do!

 El Meaningless Rewardo will try to distract you with prizes that take away from the good feelings you get.

Not today! It feels good to do my best.

So let your inner superhero challenge and inspire you. You are a **mighty motivator**.

There is no better person for the job than me. I am a **mighty motivator**.

Imagine If...

Discovery

People get excited by different things and have different interests. One of the best ways to discover your interests is by exploring the world around you. Feeling curious and trying new things can help you find what you love to do. *Imagine if you could discover more about the world around you . . .*

1. What are you capable of and enjoy doing now?

2. What is something new you would like to try?

Am I Happy With It?

My grandfather asked how I felt about the picture I drew. I was happy with it, but I still wanted more. I wanted to be that superhero. It's important to feel satisfied with the work that you do. Feeling satisfied means you feel like the job is completely done. *Imagine if after every time you did something you asked yourself, "Am I happy with it?" . . .*

1. Would you feel satisfied? Would you feel like the job is completely done?

2. If you don't feel happy with it, what should you do?

For additional tips and reference information, visit www.MVPKids.com.

Stay Away, Villains!

It's easy for failure, laziness, and rewards to take away our motivation. The fear of failing might stop us from trying. Laziness might make us miss out on great opportunities. Meaningless rewards might make us feel satisfied when the job isn't actually done. *Imagine if you were trying something new . . .*

1. What would happen if you let these distractions stop you?

2. How can you keep Professor Failure, Dr. Lazy Stryker, and El Meaningless Rewardo from squashing your motivation?

Mighty Motivator

You are a mighty motivator. You are capable of great things. If you let your inner superhero challenge and inspire you, there is so much that you can do! Sometimes there will be work, like chores and homework, that you won't feel motivated to do. *Imagine if there is a job that needs to get done that you don't want to do . . .*

1. What do you think a superhero would say about doing chores and homework?

2. How can you wake up the superhero in you to help you get the job done well?

Meet the

featured in
The Superhero in You™
with their family

Gabby González

Señor Miguel González
Abuelo / Grandfather

Señora Maria González
Abuela / Grandmother

Señor Fernando González
Papá / Father

Señora Maria Camilla González
Mamá / Mother

Verónica González
Hermanita / Little Sister

Our **Mighty Tokens**™ paperback series for Pre-K to Grade 2 helps emerging readers learn positive concepts with an experienced reader. Parents or mentors read one side of the page and children read the other side. Each book deposits tokens of affirmation into children so that they may someday become mighty adults.

Board Books

Paperbacks

Ages 0-6

Ages 4-8

Our **Celebrate!™** series focus on social and emotional needs. Helpful Teaching Tips are included in each book to equip parents, teachers, and counselors. Also available are expertly written curriculum and interactive story apps.

Ages 4-10

The **Playful Apprentice™** series is an imaginative view into children's role-playing. These picture books show a variety of community roles and career options that fuel dreams and support character building. Readers will be inspired by interviews and advice from real professionals!

Early Elementary
Ages 4-10

Our **Help Me Become™** series for early elementary readers tells three short stories of our MVP Kids® inspiring character growth. Each story concludes with a discussion guide to help the child process the story and apply the concepts.

Elementary
Ages 6-12

Our **Help Me Understand™** series for elementary readers shares the stories of our MVP Kids® learning to understand and manage a specific emotion. Readers will gain tools to take responsibility for their own emotions and develop healthy relationships.

Ages 10 and up

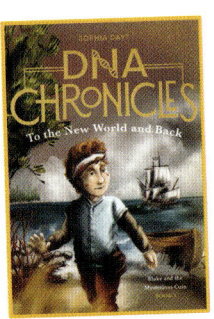

Step back in time with **DNA Chronicles™**, our historical fiction adventure series. Our MVP Kids® weave together the past and the present, reliving actual historical events to experience the history and culture of their ancestors. In these chapter books, readers will learn about the desire and fortitude it takes to commit to life's most important values, life skills, and accomplishments.

Learn more about our characters, books, puppets, SEL programs, apps, and more at **www.MVPKids.com**.

Ages 4-8

Our **Mighty Tokens™** paperback series helps emerging readers learn positive concepts with an experienced reader. Parents and mentors read one side of the page and children read the other side. Each book deposits tokens of affirmation into children so that they may someday become mighty adults.

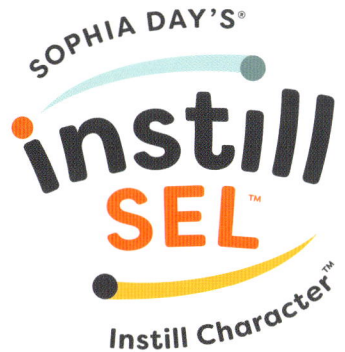

SOPHIA DAY'S® instill SEL™
Instill Character™

Social Emotional Learning (SEL) Program for Early Learners

- Entire year's worth of SEL lesson plans
- 8 MVP Kids® puppets
- Audio tracks and many more resources to build a classroom full of MVP Kids®!
- Find more information at **www.MVPKidsED.com**